A Guide to
Eastern Hawk Watching

Donald S. Heintzelm

D0800631

Keystone Books

The Pennsylvania State University Press

University Park and London

For Robert and Anne MacClay

Copyright © 1976 The Pennsylvania State University
All rights reserved

Designed by Glenn Ruby

Printed in the United States of America

Library of Congress Cataloging in Publication Data

Heintzelman, Donald S
    A guide to eastern hawk watching.

    A revision of the author's work privately pub-
lished in 1972 under title: A guide to northeastern
hawk watching.
    Includes index.
    Bibliography
    1. Birds of prey—Northeastern states. 2. Birds
of prey—Southern states. 3. Bird watching—Northeastern states. 4. Bird watching—Southern states.
I. Title.
QL696. F3H45 1976   598.9′1   76-2002
ISBN 0-271-01222-6

Preface

Most hawks, eagles, and falcons are large, powerful, and spectacular. The sight of any one of these magnificent birds is a memorable experience for every birder. Hence a visit to one of the excellent hawk lookouts in the eastern half of the United States or Canada always is a noteworthy event during the spring and autumn migration seasons. Indeed, increasing numbers of birders now plan special field trips to hawk lookouts in the hope of seeing large numbers of Broad-winged, Sharp-shinned, or Red-tailed Hawks. Some enthusiasts visit lookouts such as Bake Oven Knob and Hawk Mountain, Pennsylvania, weekend after weekend hoping to see rare and spectacular birds such as Golden Eagles, Bald Eagles, and Peregrine Falcons. These birders know that hawk watching requires persistence; one must be willing to spend long hours on the lookouts. But the results are worthwhile and thousands of people have enjoyed their first views of eagles, or other rare species, after such tireless vigils. Do not despair if you are disappointed on your first trip. Even experts sometimes predict good hawk flights and are disappointed. Experienced hawk watchers have a favorite expression—"You should have been here yesterday!"

Since the private publication in 1972 of an early version of this guide, under the title *A Guide to Northeastern Hawk Watching,* the public's interest in hawks and their migrations has continued to increase. No similar guide previously had been published for North American birds of prey despite the need for one. It was my intent to provide in a small volume information on hawk identification beyond the scope of that included in standard guides to bird identification, basic details of the migration season, and descriptions and directions for reaching a variety of good hawk lookouts.

Publication of the northeastern hawk watching guide also emphasized the need for a more detailed and comprehensive book which would compile, organize, and summarize the considerable volume of published and unpublished information on autumn hawk migrations in eastern North America. In 1973, I completed *Autumn Hawk Flights: The Migrations in Eastern North America* (Rutgers University Press, 1975). Although of great interest to most hawk watchers, the volume nonetheless goes far beyond the scope of information normally presented in a field guide. Hence, because there still is a need for a good field guide to hawk watching, it seems useful and appropriate to revise and expand the scope of the original northeastern hawk watching guide. The revisions in both text and illustrations are extensive. Among the books which were consulted frequently, in addition to *A Guide to Northeastern Hawk Watching* and *Autumn Hawk Flights,* are Brett and Nagy's *Feathers in the Wind,* Broun's *Hawks Aloft,* Peterson's *A Field Guide to the Birds,* Pough's *Audubon Water Bird Guide: Water, Game and*

Large Land Birds, Robbins' *Birds of North America,* Stone's *Bird Studies at Old Cape May,* and Porter, Willis, Christensen, and Nielsen's *Flight Identification of European Raptors.*

Much valuable information also was extracted from the periodical literature, particularly from files of *American Birds, Atlantic Naturalist, Audubon, Auk, Bulletin Massachusetts Audubon Society, California Condor, Cassinia, Cleveland Bird Calendar, Delaware Conservationist, EBBA News, Jack-Pine Warbler, Journal Hawk Migration Association North America, Journal Wildlife Management, Kingbird, Migrant, New Jersey Nature News, New Jersey State Museum Science Notes, Raptor Research News, Redstart, Search, Urner Field Observer,* and the *Wilson Bulletin.*

A number of people sent me unpublished information to which I referred in preparing this revision of the guide: G. N. Appell, Richard C. Bollinger, Norman Bowers, Tom Davis, Lucy Duncan, Carl L. Garner, William N. Grigg, Theodore R. Hake, Neil Henderson, Edwin H. Horning, Alice H. Kelley, William A. Klamm, D. L. Knohr, Robert and Anne MacClay, John P. Perkins, Elizabeth W. Phinney, Noble Proctor, D. M. Ross, Fred Scott, Robert W. Smart, and Mary Ann Sunderlin.

The following individuals contributed photographs which add significantly to the value of this guide: Alan Brady, Karl-Erik Fridzén, Harry Goldman, Karl L. Maslowski, Walter R. Spofford, Tommy Swindell, and Fred Tilly.

Some of the field data forms reproduced in Appendix 2 are printed with the permission of Andrew Bihun, Jr., and the Montclair Bird Club and James J. Brett and the Hawk Mountain Sanctuary Association.

Special appreciation also is due Mrs. Helen Poole and Joseph Poole for granting permission to use several pen and ink sketches of hawks drawn by the late Earl L. Poole. Some of these previously appeared in Richard Pough's *Audubon Water Bird Guide* published by Doubleday and Company, Inc.

Allentown, Pa.   Donald S. Heintzelman
28 April 1976

•

Checklist of Eastern Hawks

( )   Turkey Vulture

( )   Black Vulture

( )   White-tailed Kite

( )   Mississippi Kite

( )   Swallow-tailed Kite

( )   Everglade Kite

( )   Goshawk

( )   Sharp-shinned Hawk

( )   Cooper's Hawk

( )   Red-tailed Hawk

( )   Red-shouldered Hawk

( )   Broad-winged Hawk

( )   Short-tailed Hawk

( )   Swainson's Hawk

( )   Rough-legged Hawk

( )   Golden Eagle

( )   Bald Eagle

( )   Marsh Hawk

( )   Osprey

( )   Caracara

( )   Gyrfalcon

( )   Peregrine Falcon

( )   Merlin

( )   American Kestrel

Contents

Hawk Identification   9

New World Vultures: Cathartidae   9
Kites, Hawks, Harriers, Eagles: Accipitridae   10
Ospreys: Pandionidae   15
Caracaras and Falcons: Falconidae   15

Plates   17

Field Equipment   53

Binoculars   53
Telescopes   53
Decoys   53
Field Clothing   53
Other Equipment   54

The Migration Seasons   55

Spring Hawk Migrations   55
Autumn Hawk Migrations   55

Mechanics of Hawk Flights   58

General Weather Conditions   58
Updrafts   59
Thermals   59
Diversion-Lines   60

The Hawk Lookouts   62

Great Lakes Region and Eastern Canada   62

Minnesota   62
Wisconsin   63
Michigan   63
Ohio   64
Pennsylvania   66
New York   67
Ontario   67
Nova Scotia   69

New England   70

Maine   70
New Hampshire   70
Vermont   71

Massachusetts   72
Connecticut   73

Middle Atlantic States   74

New York   74
New Jersey   76
Pennsylvania   80
Maryland   86
Delaware   86
Virginia   87
West Virginia   88

Southern Appalachian States   90

Tennessee   90
Kentucky   91
North Carolina   91
Florida   91

Appendix 1   Raptor Conservation Organizations   92
Appendix 2   Sample Field Data Forms   93
Selected Reading   97
Index   98

Hawk Identification

Many birders consider diurnal birds of prey (vultures, kites, hawks, eagles, harriers, Ospreys, Caracaras, and falcons) as being difficult to identify. They are placed along with fall wood warblers and immature sparrows in that aloof category of species for which there are no quick or easy methods of becoming skilled at field identification. Nonetheless, many subtle points of diurnal raptor identification now are known and can be helpful in aiding birders to identify hawks correctly.

New World Vultures: Cathartidae

Two species of vultures occur in eastern North America. The Turkey Vulture is the common species in the northeast and the Great Lakes region. The Black Vulture is common in the southern states, but only occasionally ventures into the northeastern and Great Lakes states.

TURKEY VULTURE   *Cathartes aura*

Wingspread: 72 inches.
Field Recognition: Large, nearly eagle-size and eagle-like black birds. The wings are partly grayish or silvery on the undersides, giving the birds a two-toned appearance. The wings are held in a V or dihedral. The head is naked (red in adults and grayish-black in immatures and sub-adults) and frequently hangs down rather than extending forward. The tail is relatively long and extends well beyond the rear edge of the wings; the tip is rounded.
Flight Style: They frequently rock or tilt from side to side while soaring. The occasional wingbeats are powerful but appear labored.
Spring Migration: January, February, March.
Autumn Migration: August, September, OCTOBER, NOVEMBER.

BLACK VULTURE   *Coragyps atratus*

Wingspread: 54 to 60 inches.
Field Recognition: Large black birds with whitish patches on the undersides of the wings near the tip. The tail is short, barely extending beyond the rear edge of the wings; the tip is square. The naked head is blackish-gray.
Flight Style: Several rapid flaps, then a short sail.
Spring Migration: Resident in the South; stragglers appear in the North occasionally. April, May, June.
Autumn Migration: Northern stragglers drift southward during September, October, and November.

Kites, Hawks, Harriers, Eagles: Accipitridae

The majority of the species observed at the hawk lookouts is contained in this family. Kites rarely are seen other than in the southern states. The remaining species are diverse in habits and structure and are grouped into several subfamilies.

WHITE-TAILED KITE *Elanus leucurus*

Wingspread: 40 inches.
Field Recognition: White with black shoulders and grayish wings. The undersides of the body and wings are white, with a dark wrist patch. The wings are pointed. The whitish tail is long. The head and body of immatures are streaked with brown.
Flight Style: Gull-like with the tips of the wings pointed downward. Frequently hovers.
Spring Migration: None.
Autumn Migration: None.

MISSISSIPPI KITE *Ictinia misisippiensis*

Wingspread: 34 to 37 inches.
Field Recognition: Falcon-like with long, pointed wings. Head pale gray. Back and upperside of wings dark gray. Underparts paler. Tail black. Immatures streaked heavily with brown on the undersides.
Flight Style: Graceful and almost swallow-like. Frequently seen in flocks.
Spring Migration: March, April, May. No regular migration. Primarily restricted to the southern states although stragglers rarely appear in the northeast.
Autumn Migration: September. No regular migration. Primarily restricted to the southern states.

SWALLOW-TAILED KITE *Elanoides forficatus*

Wingspread: 45 to 50 inches.
Field Recognition: Head and underparts of the body are white. The tail, flight feathers of the wings, and the back are dark gray. The tail is deeply forked.
Flight Style: Graceful and buoyant.
Spring Migration: March, April, May. Mainly in the southern states. Stragglers occasionally occur in the North.
Autumn Migration: September. Mainly in the South.

EVERGLADE KITE   *Rostrhamus sociabilis*

Wingspread: 44 to 45 inches.
Field Recognition: Males are black with a whitish basal area on the square-tipped tail. Females are buffy and streaked heavily. They have a whitish band on the tail, and a white eyebrow. The subspecies in Florida is endangered and nearly extinct.
Flight Style: "Floppy" unlike other kites.
Migration: None. Confined (in the U.S.) to southern Florida.

GOSHAWK   *Accipiter gentilis*

Wingspread: 40 to 47 inches
Field Recognition: Adults are bluish-gray or gray on the upperparts and pale grayish-white on their undersides with darker streaks. The dark cap and cheek and the white eyebrow line are distinctive. Immatures are brown on their upperparts and whitish on their undersides with heavy brown streaking. The wings are relatively short and rounded but proportionally a little longer than the other accipiters. The tail is long and the tip is slightly to moderately rounded. Sometimes shows conspicuous white undertail coverts.
Flight Style: Several moderately rapid wingbeats, then a brief period of sailing, followed by more wingbeats.
Spring Migration: MARCH, April.
Autumn Migration: September, OCTOBER, NOVEMBER, December.

SHARP-SHINNED HAWK   *Accipiter striatus*

Wingspread: 20 to 27 inches.
Field Recognition: Adults are bluish-gray on their upperparts and whitish with reddish-brown bars on their undersides. Immatures are brown above and white below with brown streaks. The wings are short and rounded. The tip of the long tail either is square, slightly rounded, or slightly notched.
Flight Style: Several rapid wingbeats, then a brief period of sailing, followed by more wingbeats.
Spring Migration: March, APRIL, May.
Autumn Migration: August, September, OCTOBER, November.

COOPER'S HAWK   *Accipiter cooperii*

Wingspread: 27 to 36 inches.
Field Recognition: Similar to the Sharp-shinned Hawk but generally larger. The tip of the tail is extremely rounded.
Flight Style: Similar to the Sharp-shinned Hawk but a little slower.
Spring Migration: March, April, May.
Autumn Migration: September, OCTOBER, November.

RED-TAILED HAWK   *Buteo jamaicensis*

Wingspread: 46 to 58 inches.
Field Recognition: A typical soaring hawk with broad wings and tail. Extremely variable in color. Adults are brown above and white below, with a vivid reddish tail (lighter on the underside) and a conspicuous dark belly band. Seen head-on, the light cere at the base of the bill and a light wrist area on the leading edge of each wing frequently produce "headlights" which are visible at a considerable distance.
Flight Style: Frequently soars on partly folded wings on updrafts along mountains and bluffs, with wingbeats used only occasionally. The tail usually is not spread. Occasionally they circle in thermals and then completely spread their wings and tail. At times they also hover briefly, or hang motionless in mid-air, while hunting.
Spring Migration: MARCH, APRIL, May.
Autumn Migration: September, OCTOBER, NOVEMBER, December.

RED-SHOULDERED HAWK   *Buteo lineatus*

Wingspread: 32½ to 50 inches.
Field Recognition: A moderately sized soaring hawk. Adults have reddish shoulder patches on the uppersides of their wings, "windows" (areas of translucense) near the wrist, richly colored reddish underparts, and a vividly banded black and white tail. Immatures are heavily streaked on their undersides, lack a belly band, and have "windows" on their wings.
Flight Style: Fluttering wingbeats often followed by a brief sail. More or less suggests an accipiter's flight.
Spring Migration: MARCH, April.
Autumn Migration: September, OCTOBER, November.

BROAD-WINGED HAWK   *Buteo platypterus*

Wingspread: 32 to 39 inches.
Field Recognition: A chunky, crow-sized soaring hawk. Adults have two white and two black tail bands. Immatures are streaked with brown on their undersides, but are smaller and more chunky than immatures of other eastern buteos. A large light area (the cere) behind the bill suggests a "headlight" when the hawk is seen head-on. When soaring or gliding on updrafts along mountains, the wings sometimes are held in a slightly bowed position.
Flight Style: During migration, Broad-wings frequently "kettle" or flock in large numbers in thermals, then glide to new thermals, and repeat the process. No other eastern hawks form these characteristic kettles (in the western states Swainson's Hawks do so).
Spring Migration: APRIL, May.
Autumn Migration: August, SEPTEMBER, October.

SHORT-TAILED HAWK   *Buteo brachyurus*

Wingspread: 35 inches.
Field Recognition: A small (crow-sized) hawk occurring in light and dark color phases. Light phase birds are white below but are dark on the head and back. Dark phase birds are black below with a conspicuous white area on the underside of each wing; they are dark on the head and back, too. Individuals in both color phases have a black tail with three white bands. Immatures are buffy and resemble immature Broad-winged Hawks.
Flight Style: Soars on motionless wings. They may hang motionless, then stoop, when hunting.
Migration: Confined entirely within Florida. The hawks occur in the central and southern part of the state (rarely in northern Florida) from late February through early October. From mid-October through early February the population apparently migrates southward to the extreme southern part of the Florida mainland, with substantial numbers wintering within and close to Everglades National Park. The entire population of the Short-tailed Hawk in Florida numbers only about 200 birds, and the species officially is designated as rare within the United States.

SWAINSON'S HAWK   *Buteo swainsoni*

Wingspread: 47 to 57 inches.
Field Recognition: Occurs in two color phases. Light phase adults are most common. The chest, back, head, and primaries are dark and contrast with the otherwise light body and throat. Dark phase adults are rare. They are entirely blackish except for the light throat and forehead and somewhat cloudy or dark buffy undersides of the wings. The tail on birds in both color phases is light with numerous narrow, dark bands and a wider, dark subterminal band. Immatures are brown above, and white below with a brown chest and much brown streaking.
Flight Style: Kettles in large flocks during migration. When soaring the wings form a slight dihedral.
Spring Migration: April, May.
Autumn Migration: September, October.
Note: Swainson's Hawks are extremely rare in the East, but a few individuals have been observed during the spring and autumn in recent years. Sometimes these birds occur in kettles of Broad-winged Hawks.

ROUGH-LEGGED HAWK   *Buteo lagopus*

Wingspread: 48 to 56 inches.
Field Recognition: Variable in color. Dark phase birds are black with much white on the undersides of each wing. Light phase birds have a black wrist patch on each wing, a black belly, and a dark, broad band near the end of the white tail. The wings and tail are a little longer than other eastern buteos.
Flight Style: Soars on updrafts with some flapping. Frequently hovers while hunting.
Spring Migration: MARCH, April.
Autumn Migration: October, NOVEMBER.

GOLDEN EAGLE   *Aquila chrysaetos*

Wingspread: 75 to 94 inches.
Field Recognition: Adults are large dark brown birds (black at a distance). Under favorable circumstances, and at close range, the golden nape feathers can be seen. Some adults have a faint whitish-buffy base of the tail. Juveniles, immatures, and sub-adults have a large, conspicuous white patch on each wing and a broad white basal tail band. The youngest birds show the most amount of white on the wings and tail. Some individuals of the eastern Appalachian population have a whitish area on the leading edge of each wing near the wrist.
Flight Style: Soars on updrafts on broad wings, with a slight dihedral. The occasional wingbeats are powerful and labored.
Spring Migration: Probably March, April, May.
Autumn Migration: September, OCTOBER, NOVEMBER, December.

BALD EAGLE   *Haliaeetus leucocephalus*

Wingspread: 72 to 98 inches.
Field Recognition: Adults are unmistakable with their dark body and white head and tail. Immatures and sub-adults are variable but generally are dark brown (black at a distance) and can be confused with adult (and even immature and sub-adult) Golden Eagles. However, the white on the underside of each wing extends outward continually from the body toward the wingtips.
Flight Style: Similar to the Golden Eagle. Seen head-on, the wings may be held a little more level whereas the Golden Eagle may show a very slight dihedral in its flight profile.
Spring Migration: Probably February, March, April, May.
Autumn Migration: August, SEPTEMBER, October, November, December.

MARSH HAWK   *Circus cyaneus*

Wingspread: 40 to 54 inches.
Field Recognition: Individuals of all ages have a conspicuous white rump patch. Adult males are ashy-gray on their upperparts, white with some rufous on their undersides, and have black wingtips. Adult females are brown on their upperparts and lighter brown and streaked on their undersides. Immatures (both sexes) resemble adult females but their cinnamon-colored undersides are unstreaked. The long wings frequently form a slight dihedral; the wingtips sometimes appear somewhat pointed or rounded.
Flight Style: Unsteady; frequently rocks, tips, and zigzags on updrafts. Also quarters low over marshes.
Spring Migration: March, APRIL, May.
Autumn Migration: August, September, OCTOBER, November.

Ospreys: Pandionidae

The one species of Osprey or Fish Hawk occurs widely throughout the world. It has seriously declined in numbers in some areas including many parts of North America.

OSPREY   *Pandion haliaetus*

Wingspread: 54 to 72 inches.
Field Recognition: A large hawk, dark brown above and white below. A black patch extends through the cheeks and eyes and contrasts with the white head. The wings frequently are bent deeply or crooked, and have a black wrist. Sometimes confused with Bald Eagles.
Flight Style: Soars on updrafts with deeply bent or crooked wings—extremely characteristic. The wings appear bowed when seen head-on. Commonly hovers over water.
Spring Migration: March, APRIL, May.
Autumn Migration: August, SEPTEMBER, October, November.

Caracaras and Falcons: Falconidae

Caracaras, although related to falcons, nonetheless are rather terrestrial birds and are more vulture-like than falcon-like in their habits. Falcons are long-winged hawks with pointed wingtips and long tails. They are very streamlined birds with a direct and rapid flight. Generally they prefer open areas and coastal migration routes, but some individuals migrate along the Appalachian ridges and the shorelines of the Great Lakes.

CARACARA   *Caracara cheriway*

Wingspread: 48 inches.
Field Recognition: A long-legged scavenger distributed locally in Florida's open scrublands and prairies. On the ground it is distinguished by its red face, black crest, dark wings and body, large white head and throat, and long white tail with a dark terminal band. In flight it has a large light patch on each wing near the tip. Caracaras commonly associate with vultures.
Flight Style: Resembles a Marsh Hawk's flight style—irregular or zigzagging but with rapid wingbeats then long periods of sailing. The appearance is swift and graceful.
Migration: None.

GYRFALCON   *Falco rusticolus*

Wingspread: 44 to 52 inches.
Field Recognition: A very large black, gray, or white falcon. Immatures

show much streaking on their undersides. The wingtips are slightly rounded compared with the smaller falcons. When soaring the wings usually are slightly bowed or held level; occasionally a dihedral is noticeable.

Flight Style: Slow, gull-like wingbeats as if made entirely by the hands but the flight is deceptively fast.

Spring Migration: Through April; no specific months.

Autumn Migration: October, November; no specific months.

Note: Gyrfalcons are *extremely rare* south of Canada. They are more likely to appear at the Great Lakes lookouts.

PEREGRINE FALCON   *Falco peregrinus*

Wingspread: 38 to 46 inches.

Field Recognition: A crow-sized falcon. Adults are slaty-backed and dark capped with distinctive "sideburns" and barred undersides. Immatures are brown and heavily streaked on their undersides. Identify Peregrines with extreme care. They are endangered and rarely seen.

Flight Style: Fast with quick "rowing" wingbeats. Seldom soars.

Spring Migration: March, April, May.

Autumn Migration: August, September, OCTOBER, November.

MERLIN   *Falco columbarius*

Wingspread: 23½ to 26½ inches.

Field Recognition: A small, dark, jay-sized falcon. Adult males have bluish-gray upperparts but lighter underparts with some streaks. The tail is banded conspicuously. Adult females and immatures are brown with heavily streaked underparts. Somewhat suggests a miniature Peregrine *without* "sideburns."

Flight Style: Swift and direct with "rowing" wingbeats. Frequently flies low over the ground or just above treetops.

Spring Migration: March, April, May.

Autumn Migration: September, OCTOBER, November.

AMERICAN KESTREL   *Falco sparverius*

Wingspread: 20 to 24½ inches.

Field Recognition: Our smallest and most colorful falcon (robin-sized). Both sexes have a rusty back, two "sideburns" or "whiskers" on each side of the head, and a rufous-reddish tail. Males have bluish-gray wings; females have brownish wings.

Flight Style: Buoyant and less rapid than the intermediate sized falcons, with occasional periods of gliding or soaring between wingbeats. Frequently hovers when hunting, but rarely does so (hovers) while migrating. Sometimes the wings are folded into a sickle shape.

Spring Migration: MARCH, April, May.

Autumn Migration: August, SEPTEMBER, October, November.

Plates

Turkey Vulture

F.T.

F.T.

Illustration Credits: A. Brady, K. E. Fridzén, H. Goldman, D. S. Heintzelman, K. H. Maslowski, E. Poole, W. R. Spofford, F. Tilly.

Turkey Vulture

D.S.H.

D.S.H.

Black Vulture

D.S.H.

D.S.H.

Kites

White-tailed Kite

Swallow-tailed Kite

Kites

Mississippi Kite

Everglade Kite

Goshawk

Adult

Adult

Goshawk

Adult

Immature

Cooper's Hawk

Sharp-shinned Hawk

F.T.

F.T.

Sharp-shinned Hawk

D.S.H.

D.S.H.

27

Sharp-shinned Hawk

D.S.H.

F.T.

Red-tailed Hawk

A.B.

F.T.

Red-tailed Hawk

D.S.H.

F.T.

Broad-winged Hawks

A.B.

D.S.H.

Rarer Buteos

Short-tailed Hawk — dark phase

Dark Phase

Light Phase

Swainson's Hawk

Rarer Buteos

K.H.M.

Rough-legged Hawk — light phase

H.G.

Rough-legged Hawk — light phase

Rarer Buteos

Rough-legged Hawk — dark phase

Rough-legged Hawk — dark phase

Bald Eagle

Adult

Adult

Bald Eagle

Immature

Immature

Golden Eagle

W.R.S.

W.R.S.

Adult

Juvenile

41

Marsh Hawk

H.G.

Adult male

F.T.

Adult male

42

Marsh Hawk

H.G.

Adult female

F.T.

Marsh Hawk

F.T.

Immature

D.S.H.

Immature

44

Osprey

D.S.H.

D.S.H.

Osprey

D.S.H.

Osprey

D.S.H.

Caracara

E.P.

Larger Falcons

K.E.F.

Gyrfalcon

K.E.F.

Gyrfalcon

48

Larger Falcons

K.H.M.

Peregrine Falcon

W.R.S.

Peregrine Falcon

Smaller Falcons

Merlin

American Kestrel

Smaller Falcons

D.S.H.

American Kestrel

D.S.H.

American Kestrel

51

Smaller Falcons

American Kestrel

American Kestrel

Field Equipment

Selection of the correct field equipment is essential for successful and enjoyable hawk watching. The items listed here are particularly useful to casual birders who are interested mainly in seeing migrating hawks. Persons planning serious studies of hawk migrations will find additional types of field equipment necessary. These are discussed in more detail in *Autumn Hawk Flights*.

Binoculars

Good binoculars are necessary for watching migrating hawks, and visitors to lookouts in the East use a wide assortment of brands and types. For occasional hawk watching standard 7x35, 7x50, or 8x40 birding binoculars are adequate. But if detailed field studies are planned as part of a research project, most experienced hawk watchers prefer 10X binoculars because they frequently permit more rapid and accurate hawk identification.

Telescopes

It also is very useful to have a telescope available at a hawk lookout in order to identify birds flying at a distance or under dim light conditions. An instrument equipped with a 20X eyepiece is adequate. If few people are present on a lookout, the telescope can be mounted on a tripod for support. However, most experienced observers prefer to mount their telescopes on gunstocks if they intend to visit one of the more popular lookouts which frequently are very crowded with visitors. Scopes mounted on gunstocks also are more maneuverable

Decoys

Many hawk watchers place a papier-mâché Great Horned Owl on a long pole in an upright position at the lookouts they visit. Some species of hawks, e.g., Goshawks and Sharp-shinned and Cooper's Hawks, are attracted to decoys and dart within a few feet of both decoys and observers. These can be among the most exciting and memorable experiences resulting from a visit to a lookout.

Field Clothing

The weather conditions prevailing at the eastern hawk lookouts are extremely variable and they dictate the type of field clothing which is suitable or necessary. For example, air temperatures sometimes soar into the nineties during August and September, but sub-freezing temperatures are not uncommon at some lookouts during November and early December. Therefore, it is extremely important to dress correctly.

Whenever in doubt carry an extra jacket or sweater with you. A cap for protection from the sun, or a hood during the colder part of the season, also is recommended. Normal hiking boots or shoes with rubber soles are ideal. Gloves, too, are necessary during cold weather. Some hawk watchers also put a raincoat or poncho into their packs.

Other Equipment

A pack frame, knapsack, or other field pack or bag is very useful when visiting a lookout because lunches, thermos, field guides, cameras, and other items can be carried easily while allowing free use of the hands. A small pillow or cushion also is useful to sit on since many mountain lookouts are covered with rocks or boulders. An aluminum beach chair can be taken to lookouts which are easily approached, such as Cape May Point, New Jersey, but such chairs are not recommended for lookouts in more remote areas because of the difficulty of carrying them and the crowds of people which gather at some of these spots.

It always is helpful to carry a small notebook or checklist on which to record the hawks and other birds you have seen. Special field data forms also are used in research projects (samples are found in Appendix 2). Lunch and a beverage must be taken to most lookouts since it is impossible to buy food or beverages at most sites.

Goshawk attacking an artificial owl decoy. Photo by F. Tilly.

The Migration Seasons

Hawk migrations in eastern North America occur during fairly well defined temporal periods in spring and autumn and are related to weather conditions, geographic features, and other less obvious factors.

Spring Hawk Migrations

The northward spring hawk migrations in the East are not nearly as spectacular or concentrated in most locations as are the famous autumn flights. Nonetheless, large spring flights can be seen at a few lookouts—particularly along the southern shorelines of Lakes Erie and Ontario—and modest flights also occur at a number of other locations including many important autumn lookouts. In general, however, the spring hawk flights are more dispersed than autumn flights.

March, April, and May are the most important months for watching spring hawk migrations with mid- to late April being especially important. Sometimes flights of several thousand Broad-winged Hawks are seen during a single day during that period along the southern shoreline of Lake Ontario. In the Great Lakes region, the best concentration spots seem to be located where fingers of land extend into the lake a short distance west of the lookout.

Autumn Hawk Migrations

The autumn hawk migrations in eastern North America are among the most extraordinary animal spectacles in the world. For more than three months tens of thousands of vultures, hawks, eagles, harriers, Ospreys, and falcons follow the coastlines, mountain ridges, and Great Lakes shorelines southward en route to their ancestral wintering grounds. As they do so, they offer birders, naturalists, and other people exceptional opportunities to observe and enjoy these flights at scores of lookouts. To increasingly large numbers of out-of-doors minded people, watching autumn hawk flights is a highlight of the year's activities—a time to be looked forward to with keen anticipation.

The autumn hawk migration season extends from early August through early December, but the bulk of the flights occur from September through November. Within this three month period, the season can be further divided into three major segments based upon the peak migration periods of Broad-winged Hawks, Sharp-shinned Hawks, and Red-tailed Hawks. These are the three most abundant species seen at the hawk lookouts.

September is noted for Broad-winged Hawk flights which frequently peak about the middle of the month. Such flights, which sometimes contain many thousands of hawks, invariably occur between 11 and 24 September, with 16 or 17 September often producing exceptional flights. At Hawk Mountain Sanctuary, Pennsylvania, for example, 11,392 hawks (mainly

Spring Hawk Flights

Species	March	April	May
GOSHAWK			
SHARP-SHINNED HAWK			
COOPER'S HAWK			
RED-TAILED HAWK			
RED-SHOULDERED HAWK			
BROAD-WINGED HAWK			
ROUGH-LEGGED HAWK			
GOLDEN EAGLE			
BALD EAGLE			
MARSH HAWK			
OSPREY			
PEREGRINE FALCON			
MERLIN			
AMERICAN KESTREL			

Fall Hawk Flights

Species	September	October	November
TURKEY VULTURE			
GOSHAWK			
SHARP-SHINNED HAWK			
COOPER'S HAWK			
RED-TAILED HAWK			
RED-SHOULDERED HAWK			
BROAD-WINGED HAWK			
ROUGH-LEGGED HAWK			
GOLDEN EAGLE			
BALD EAGLE			
MARSH HAWK			
OSPREY			
PEREGRINE FALCON			
MERLIN			
AMERICAN KESTREL			

The relative abundance of each species during a particular month is indicated by the thickness of each line.

Broad-wings) were counted on 16 September 1948, and similar or larger counts have been recorded at lookouts in New Jersey and at various sites along the northern shorelines of Lakes Erie and Superior.

In addition to September's spectacular Broad-wing flights, Bald Eagles also migrate southward in small numbers during late August and throughout September, with occasional stragglers appearing as late as early December. Ospreys also are notable components of the September hawk flights, largest numbers appearing during mid- to late September. On 11 September 1965, for example, a flight of 102 Ospreys passed Bake Oven Knob, Pennsylvania.

October forms the second major period in the autumn hawk flights. Sharp-shinned Hawks are the most abundant migrants from early to mid-October, but they become less numerous later in the month. Adding zest to the season, however, are lesser numbers of other species including Goshawks, Cooper's Hawks, Golden Eagles, Marsh Hawks, Peregrine Falcons, Merlins, and American Kestrels. On 16 October 1970, at Cape May Point, New Jersey, for example, an extraordinary flight of about 25,000 kestrels was seen! In addition to hawks, thousands of Canada Geese also are seen during October at the hawk lookouts. Thrushes, kinglets, vireos, wood warblers, blackbirds and grackles, and sparrows also flood the skies and woodlands at hawk lookouts during October.

Toward the end of October and continuing into November, the largest and most majestic hawks reach peaks of abundance in their southward migrations. Pick any cold day with northwest winds in early November and goodly numbers of Red-tailed Hawks are likely to be seen at many of the mountain lookouts. Adding more excitement to these flights are lesser numbers of Goshawks, Red-shouldered Hawks, Rough-legged Hawks, Golden Eagles, Marsh Hawks, and occasionally other species. Golden Eagles, in particular, are the highlights of the hawking season. Indeed every visitor to a hawk lookout hopes to see one of these regal birds, although less than 50 are counted each year even at the best lookouts. Nonetheless, dedicated hawk watchers can see these birds eventually if they make repeated visits to places such as Bake Oven Knob and Hawk Mountain, Pennsylvania. Perhaps you will be exceptionally lucky on your first visit and see a Golden Eagle immediately. If you select the correct day in mid- to late October or early November, it is possible to do so. If you fail on your first trip, try again. To see the King of Birds is well worth the effort!

Mechanics of Hawk Flights

In addition to knowing when to visit a hawk lookout, the chances of seeing a good hawk flight also are improved through an understanding of the basic mechanics of hawk flights. Among the most important factors are general weather conditions, local weather conditions such as updrafts and thermals, and so-called diversion-lines.

General Weather Conditions

In spring, the largest hawk flights seem to occur on southerly winds which are accompanied by a drop in barometric pressure, a rise in air temperature, and the westerly approach of a low-pressure area and a cold front.

Large autumn hawk flights also tend to occur in the wake of certain weather features. Generally a pronounced low-pressure area first covers lower New England and upstate New York followed a day or two later by the passage of a strong cold front across the East or Northeast. The front is accompanied by brisk northwest, north, or west winds. This combination of wind and weather usually provides ideal hawk flight conditions, but occasionally good flights also occur on easterly and southerly winds.

When surface winds strike the sides of mountains they are deflected up-ward. Migrating hawks soar on these updrafts.

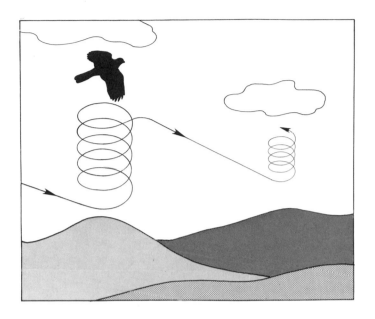

Migrating Broad-winged Hawks enter thermals, ride them aloft, then glide downward to another thermal and repeat the process.

Updrafts

The cold, brisk northwest surface winds which usually occur after the passage of a strong cold front create excellent flight conditions for migrating hawks because they strike the sides of mountains and are deflected upward. It is these updrafts or deflective air currents which are perfect for the soaring flight used extensively by buteos, accipiters, and other hawks. In addition to creating strong updrafts along the inland mountains, northwest winds also tend to concentrate hawks at certain geographic bottlenecks such as Cape May Point, New Jersey. The hawks apparently are unwilling to cross Delaware Bay unless the wind changes direction. However, they sometimes follow the New Jersey side of the bay northward until they can cross at a narrow spot despite the northwesterly winds.

Thermals

In addition to the importance of updrafts to migrating hawks, thermals (bubbles of warm air which rise into the atmosphere) also are of major importance to migrating Broad-winged Hawks. Indeed it is this dependence upon thermals which causes hundreds of Broad-wings to mass together in milling flocks called "kettles"—extraordinary spectacles which hawk watchers eagerly look forward to seeing.

In the eastern United States and Canada, Broad-winged Hawks are the only raptors which make extensive use of thermals during migration. But in the West, Swainson's Hawks also utilize thermals extensively, and both species frequently kettle in mixed flocks in Central America en route to or from their winter ranges.

The use of thermals by hawks such as Broad-wings enables these birds to migrate over vast distances while expending very little energy. This is accomplished by entering thermals and remaining in them as they rise into the atmosphere. When the warm air in the thermals begins to cool and the thermals dissipate in the form of cumulus clouds, the hawks leave and begin long, downward glides which sometimes extend for several miles until another newly formed thermal is located. Then the process is repeated. In this manner Broad-winged Hawks migrate cross-country drifting on the wind, or move down the great folds of the Appalachians, or around the shorelines of the Great Lakes, thence around the Gulf of Mexico and through Central America into their South American winter range.

Thermal soaring is one of the most effective and practical methods of flight employed by migrating hawks. Sometimes Broad-winged Hawks also use combinations of thermal and updraft soaring, as do other species, when cross-country flights are taken over mountains and valleys. At such times hawks may drift across valleys on thermals, but may change direction and use updrafts along mountains when they are encountered, before resorting to thermal soaring again.

Diversion-Lines

In various parts of eastern North America, prominent geographic features such as the shorelines of the Great Lakes, the Appalachian Mountain ridges, and the Atlantic coastline extend unbroken for relatively long distances.

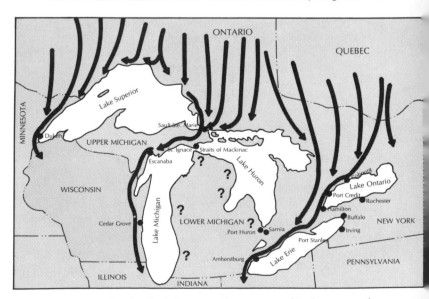

Some migrating hawks follow prominent geographic features such as shorelines of large lakes, mountain ridges, or coastlines when they are encountered. Such natural features are called diversion-lines or leading-lines.

Scientists refer to these natural features as diversion-lines or leading-lines. When soaring hawks encounter such diversion-lines during migration, they frequently divert at least a portion of their migration along such features for varying distances. For some birds, such as the Broad-winged Hawk which is especially reluctant to cross large expanses of water, the northern and western shorelines of the Great Lakes act as major autumn diversion-lines. In spring, when the hawks are migrating northward, the southern shorelines of Lakes Erie and Ontario play a similar role. Elsewhere, as along the ridges of the Appalachians, the updrafts provide extremely favorable soaring conditions for buteos and a wide assortment of other hawks. Falcons, however, are not particularly dependent upon soaring flight and they occur in much larger numbers during autumn along the Atlantic coastline rather than inland along the ridges. Many of these migrating falcons take advantage of the large numbers of small birds (which also migrate along the coast) as a readily available supply of food.

Although some scientists differ sharply in respect to the role which wind drift plays in influencing migrating hawks to use diversion-lines—some think that hawks follow them regardless of wind conditions, others because of wind conditions—in all probability a combination of both factors, particularly strong northwest winds and prominent geographic features, influence migrating hawks to utilize diversion-lines. Like many aspects of hawk migrations, however, additional field studies may produce a more refined understanding of diversion-line phenomena.

The Hawk Lookouts

Great Lakes Region and Eastern Canada

Very large autumn hawk flights occur along the northern and/or western shorelines of the Great Lakes, but less concentrated flights occur in extreme eastern Canada including the maritime provinces. Spring hawk flights in this region are confined largely to narrow flight lines along the southern shorelines of the Great Lakes—particularly Lakes Erie and Ontario.

Minnesota

Hawk Ridge Nature Reserve (Duluth)

Spring Flights: Fair.
Autumn Flights: Excellent.
Description: Bluffs rising 600 to 800 feet above the shoreline of Lake Superior in Duluth. The most important spot, the Skyline Boulevard lookout, is the shoulder of a gravel road (Skyline Parkway).
Access: In Duluth drive east on London Road to 47 Avenue East. Turn uphill, continue for a mile to Glenwood Street, turn left, and continue 0.8 mile to Skyline Parkway. Turn sharply to the right onto this gravel road and continue a mile to the Hawk Ridge Nature Reserve sign. Park along the road and observe from anywhere near the sign.
Reference: Wilson Bulletin, 1966: 79–87.

Skyline Boulevard Lookout, Hawk Ridge Nature Reserve, Duluth, Minn. Photo by D.S. Heintzelman.

Wisconsin

Cedar Grove Ornithological Station (near Cedar Grove)

Spring Flights: Fair.
Autumn Flights: Very good.
Description: A high bluff near Lake Michigan, or any spot near the lake shoreline with an unrestricted view.
Access: Drive east on U.S. Route 141 to the junction of Route 42 near Cedar Grove. Continue east on Route 141 for 0.5 mile to the point where the highway turns north. Turn onto a gravel road and continue eastward 0.25 mile toward Lake Michigan, then turn sharply north onto the first road on the left. Continue for 0.5 mile, cross Bahr Creek, and park near the sanctuary. Presumably hawk watchers are not welcome in the sanctuary but it may be possible to watch migrating hawks from the vicinity of the sanctuary itself.
Reference: Wilson Bulletin, 1961: 171–92.

Michigan

Straits of Mackinac (near Mackinac City)

Spring Flights: Good.
Autumn Flights: Fair?
Description: Details unavailable, but presumably any open spot along the Straits near Mackinac City.
Access: From the lower peninsula drive north on Interstate 75 to Mackinac City.
Reference: Jack-Pine Warbler, 1965, 43: 79–83.

Whitefish Point

Spring Flights: Good.
Autumn Flights: Fair?
Description: A parking lot near the lighthouse, the road leading to the Point, or the dunes west of the road near the shoreline.
Access: From the Lower Peninsula cross the Straits of Mackinac on Interstate 75 and continue northward to the junction of Route 123. Turn onto Route 123 and continue north to Paradise, then follow an unnumbered road north for about 12 miles to Whitefish Point.
Reference: Jack-Pine Warbler, 1965, 43: 79–83.

Ohio

Conneaut

Spring Flights: Good.
Autumn Flights: None.
Description: Open fields on the lake plain near the shoreline of Lake Erie.
Access: From Interstate 90 south of Conneaut, take the Conneaut-Andover interchange and drive north on Route 7 into Conneaut (where Route 7 becomes Mill Street). Continue to Lake Road, turn left, and continue west on Lake Road to Parrish Road. Turn left onto Parrish Road and continue to a large white barn on the west side of the street. The open fields over which hawks migrate surround the barn. Permission should be obtained to park near the barn, which is on private property.
Reference: None.

Lakewood Park (Cleveland)

Spring Flights: Good.
Autumn Flights: None.
Description: A landfill projecting into Lake Erie from which one has a fine view of bluffs toward the east and west.
Access: From Interstate 80 (south of Cleveland) drive north on Interstate 71 into the city to the junction with 130 Street. Drive north on 130 Street to Route 10 (Lorain Avenue), turn east onto Route 10 and continue to West 117 Street. Turn onto West 117 Street and continue north to Lake Avenue. Turn left (west) onto Lake Avenue and continue to the intersection of Belle Avenue. Turn right into Lakewood Park and drive to the lakefront landfill extending into the lake from which observations are made.
References: Cleveland Bird Calendar, 1962, 58(3): 28–33; 1963, 59(3): 28–31.

Perkins Beach (Cleveland)

Spring Flights: Good.
Autumn Flights: None.
Description: The top of bluffs overlooking Lake Erie, particularly the top of the rise to the right of West Boulevard.
Access: Follow the directions to Lakewood Park as far as Lake Avenue, at which point turn right (east) onto the avenue. Continue to West Boulevard (West 100 Street) then turn left (north) and continue to the lakefront and the area known formerly as Perkins Beach. Currently this is the western edge of Edgewater Park.
References: Cleveland Bird Calendar, 1962, 58(3): 28–33; 1963, 59(3): 28–31.

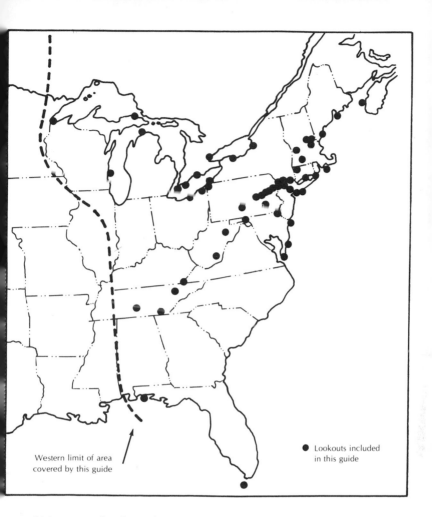

● Lookouts included
in this guide

Western limit of area
covered by this guide

Major eastern hawk watching sites.

Pennsylvania

This section on Pennsylvania hawk lookouts is restricted to those along the southern shoreline of Lake Erie. These are spring lookouts primarily. Other major lookouts in this state are discussed in the section on the Middle Atlantic States.

Lake City

Spring Flights: Good.
Autumn Flights: None.
Description: An open field with an unrestricted view to Lake Erie at the rear of the Berkeley Inn Motel.
Access: From the intersection of Routes 5 and 18, near Lake City, drive east on Route 5 for about a mile to the Berkeley Inn Motel. Observe from the area at the rear of the motel. The field over which one looks is private property and open only to foot travel, which must be confined *only* to the dirt road running down the middle of the field.
Reference: None.

Presque Isle State Park (near Erie)

Spring Flights: Fair.
Autumn Flights: None.
Description: The parking lot at Beach 10 and the shoreline of Lake Erie east of the parking lot. Alternatively, the trail starting at the Thompson Bay traffic circle and leading west along Long Ridge.
Access: From Interstate 90 drive north on Route 832 to the park entrance near Erie. Secure park maps and other information at the park administration building about a mile inside the park. Then continue to the lookout areas.
Reference: None.

West Lake Junior High School (in Erie)

Spring Flights: Good.
Autumn Flights: None.
Description: A grass slope at the rear (northwest corner) of the school. The site overlooks an expanse of open land between the school and the shoreline of Lake Erie.
Access: The school is located at 4330 West Lake Road (Pennsylvania Route 5A) in Erie. From the junction of Pennsylvania Routes 5A and 832 drive west on Route 5A for about 2 miles to the school on the north side of the highway.
Reference: None.

New York

This section on New York lookouts is confined to sites along the southern shoreline of Lake Ontario. These are spring lookouts. Additional spring and/or autumn lookouts in New York are discussed in the section on the Middle Atlantic States.

Braddock Bay State Park (Greece)

Spring Flights: Good.
Autumn Flights: None.
Description: The parking lot of the park known locally among hawk watchers as Hawk Lookout.
Access: From the Lake Ontario State Parkway on the north side of Rochester, drive west for several miles to the East Manitou Road exit ramp. Leave the parkway here and turn right at the stop sign, then drive about 500 feet to the entrance to Braddock Bay State Park. Enter the park and drive another 0.4 mile to the parking lot from which hawk watching is done.
Reference: The California Condor, 1972, 7(5): 9–10.

Derby Hill (near Mexico)

Spring Flights: Excellent.
Autumn Flights: None.
Description: An exposed field on a ridge near the shoreline of Lake Ontario.
Access: From Mexico, drive north on Route 3 for 4.5 miles to the junction of Route 104B. Turn west onto Route 104B and continue for 0.5 mile to the corner of Sage Creek Drive (marked by a barn with twin silos). Turn onto Sage Creek Drive and continue to the end. Either park here along the road or turn right up a dirt road and park at the top of the hill. Walk to the field on the right. This is only about 100 feet from a cliff overlooking Lake Ontario.
References: Kingbird, 1966, 16(1): 5–16; *Wilson Bulletin,* 1966: 88–110.

Ontario (Canada)

Hawk Cliff (near Port Stanley)

Spring Flights: None.
Autumn Flights: Excellent.
Description: Fields near the edge of a 100-foot-high cliff at the edge of Lake Erie, or a wooded ravine inland about 0.25 mile from the lake.
Access: From St. Thomas, drive south on Route 22 for about 8 miles directly to the cliffs overlooking Lake Erie.
Reference: Search, 1972, 2(16): 1–60.

Derby Hill, N.Y. Photo by D.S. Heintzelman.

Holiday Beach Provincial Park (near Windsor)

Spring Flights: None.
Autumn Flights: Excellent.
Description: A parking lot in the park next to the water.
Access: From Windsor, follow Highway 18 through Amherstburg. After crossing Big Creek continue for about 2 miles to the intersection of 18A. Turn right and continue for about 3 miles to the park entrance on the right. Enter and drive to the parking lot farthest from the park entrance. Observe from here.
Reference: American Birds, 1975, 29(1): 49–50.

Port Credit

Spring Flights: None.
Autumn Flights: Good.
Description: The vicinity of the Route 10 bridge over the Queen's Way.

Access: Drive about 15 miles southwest of Toronto on the Queen Elizabeth Way. At the junction of Provincial Route 10 turn onto it and continue to the bridge crossing the Queen's Way.
Reference: Audubon Magazine, 1962, 64(1): 44–45, 49.

Point Pelee National Park (near Leamington)

Spring Flights: None.
Autumn Flights: Excellent.
Description: The forest or open beach at the tip of the point, the vicinity of the park's Interpretive Center, or the open fields behind the maintenance compound.
Access: Drive south from Leamington for about 6 miles into the park.
References: EBBA News, 1961, 24(2): 25–26; *Wilson Bulletin,* 1966: 122.

Nova Scotia (Canada)

Brier Island (near Digby)

Spring Flights: None.
Autumn Flights: Fair to good.
Description: Open areas around either of two lighthouses. The North Point Light, in whose vicinity most observations are made, is on a rocky point 50 feet above sea level. An open area covered with heath-type vegetation surrounds the Light. The vicinity of the South Light sometimes is more productive when weather changes force hawks to stop over on Brier Island.
Access: From Digby drive on Route 217 for about 30 miles to East Ferry. Board a car ferry here (operating hourly) and cross to Long Island and the village of Tiverton. Continue on Route 217 for about 11 miles to Freeport. Here board another car ferry and cross to Westport—the only village on Brier Island. From Westport continue to the appropriate lighthouse. A good road runs from one end of the island to the other.
References: The Birds of Nova Scotia (Nova Scotia Museum, 1962); *Autumn Hawk Flights* (Rutgers University Press, 1975).

New England

Although the number of important hawk lookouts which have been discovered in New England still is relatively small, those discussed in this chapter are useful. As additional field studies continue in New England other good lookouts also may be discovered.

Maine

Acadia National Park (near Bar Harbor)

Spring Flights: None?
Autumn Flights: Fair.
Description: The exposed summit of Mount Cadillac or the flat ground between the ocean and the base of Mount Cadillac near Otter Creek.
Access: From Bar Harbor drive into the park and follow the directional signs to the site you select. Various other roads also lead into the park from other directions.
Reference: Autumn Hawk Flights (Rutgers University Press, 1975).

Casco Bay Area (near Portland)

Spring Flights: None.
Autumn Flights: Good.
Description: Detailed information on lookouts in this area is unavailable, but apparently the best hawk lookout in the Casco Bay area is located on private property near Harpswell. Presumably observations elsewhere along the shoreline of Casco Bay (particularly near the head of the bay), and on the outer islands, might produce other favorable flight lines and suitable lookouts.
Access: Various roads lead into the Casco Bay area near Portland. Refer to local road maps.
Reference: American Birds, 1974, 28(1):113–14.

New Hampshire

Little Round Top (near Bristol)

Spring Flights: None.
Autumn Flights: Good.
Description: An exposed summit of a hill with good views in all directions except toward the southwest.

Access: From the center of Bristol drive south on Route 3A to a firehouse in the middle of a fork in the road near the edge of town. Follow the right fork up a hill then turn right at the next fork. Follow this road as far as possible, ignoring all roads which turn sharply right, to the Slim Baker Conservation Area and Day Camp. Park near the main building. Then walk along a trail or old road to the lookout on the northeast corner of the top of the hill—about a ten-minute walk.

Reference: Autumn Hawk Flights (Rutgers University Press, 1975).

Peaked Hill (near New Hampton)

Spring Flights: Good.
Autumn Flights: Poor.
Description: A vista from a road overlooking large fields.
Access: From Interstate 93 near Bristol take exit 23 and follow Route 104 toward Bristol. Cross a bridge and at the next right turn onto River Road. Drive to the fork, keep right, then continue to (and take) the next *sharp left turn. Drive up the hill past the last farmhouse and stop at a cattle gate on the left. Remain on the side of the road at this spot and look over the fields on either side of the road.*
Reference: None.

Uncanoonuc Mountain (near Goffstown)

Spring Flights: None.
Autumn Flights: Good.
Description: A parking lot with visibility restricted by trees, or a fire tower if permission can be secured.
Access: From Main Street in Goffstown, drive on Mountain Road keeping left around two sharp curves at two intersections. Then turn left again onto Mountain Summit Road, following it to the top of the mountain. Park near the fire tower.
Reference: Autumn Hawk Flights (Rutgers University Press, 1975).

Vermont

Hogback Mountain (between Bennington and Brattleboro)

Spring Flights: None?
Autumn Flights: Fair.
Description: An overview beside the road with excellent views toward the south.
Access: From Bennington drive east on Route 9. The highway crosses Hogback Mountain and the overview beside the road is obvious.
Reference: Autumn Hawk Flights (Rutgers University Press, 1975).

Massachusetts

Martha's Vineyard

Spring Flights: None.
Autumn Flights: Poor.
Description: The shoreline along the southeastern end of Chappaquiddick Island and the entire southern shore of Martha's Vineyard as far as Squibnocket Point and Zacks Cliffs serve as a migration route for limited numbers of Peregrine Falcons in autumn.
Access: Various roads on the island pass within close proximity to portions of the shorelines mentioned above. Some walking and searching for favorable observation spots will be necessary. Most accommodations on the island are available by advance reservation only.
Reference: Autumn Hawk Flights (Rutgers University Press, 1975).

Mount Tom State Reservation (near Holyoke)

Spring Flights: None.
Autumn Flights: Good.
Description: Observations are made from an open steel tower on the summit of Goat Peak located within the reservation.
Access: From Interstate 91 take the East Hampton exit and follow Route 141 north for 2.3 miles to the reservation entrance. Turn right and continue 1.5 miles into the reserve to the Goat Peak parking lot. Then walk along a well used trail to the Goat Peak observation tower.
References: Bulletin Massachusetts Audubon Society, 1937, 21:5–8; 1937, 21: 5–8.

Upridge view from Goat Peak, Mount Tom State Reservation, Mass. Photo by D.S. Heintzelman.

Connecticut

Bald Peak (near Salisbury)

Spring Flights: None?
Autumn Flights: Good.
Description: A rocky ridge with a 360-degree view.
Access: From Hartford drive north on Route 44 to Salisbury (in the northwest corner of the state), then follow Mount Riga Road for about 4.1 miles to the Bald Peak parking area (about 0.3 mile beyond South Pond). Five minutes are required to walk from the parking area to a large rock ledge.
Reference: Autumn Hawk Flights (Rutgers University Press, 1975).

Lighthouse Point Park (in New Haven)

Spring Flights: Poor.
Autumn Flights: Good.
Description: A large, open field atop a knoll about 300 yards north of the park's beach.
Access: From Interstate 95 at New Haven, take exit 50 (Main St. East Haven) and, at the second traffic light, turn right onto Townsend Avenue. Continue on Townsend Avenue 2.2 miles to the traffic light at Lighthouse Point Road. Turn right and follow Lighthouse Point Road for 0.1 mile into the park. Park in the dirt parking lot, then walk north to the large field atop the knoll adjacent to the parking lot.
Reference: Auk, 1895, 12: 259–70.

Middle Atlantic States

Within the region containing the Middle Atlantic states are numerous important hawk lookouts, some among the most famous sites in the East. All of the important hawk lookouts in New York and Pennsylvania are discussed here, except those discussed in the section on the Great Lakes region.

New York

Fire Island (Robert Moses State Park near Babylon)

Spring Flights: None.
Autumn Flights: Good.
Description: The beach or dunes at Democrat Point at the western end of the island. Alternatively, on top of high dunes halfway between the eastern boundary of the park and the Fire Island lighthouse. Any narrow spot along the beach, with an unobstructed view across the width of the island, also is satisfactory.
Access: From Babylon drive east on Route 27A then south on the Robert Moses Causeway across Captree State Park and the Fire Island Inlet into Robert Moses State Park. If parking areas number four and five are open park in number five and walk eastward toward the lighthouse. If they are closed, park in area number three. To visit Democrat Point park in area number two and walk to the western end of the island.
Reference: Kingbird, 1963, 13(1): 4–12.

Fishers Island

Spring Flights: None.
Autumn Flights: Fair.
Description: The top of Mount Chocomount, about three-quarters of the way down the island, or just to the west of a small bluff near the east end of Beach Pond at Middlefarm Flats about halfway down the island.
Access: By the Fishers Island ferry boats (the Mystic Isle or the Olinda) which leave from the vicinity of the old railroad station at the foot of State Street in New London, Conn.
Reference: Auk, 1922: 488–96.

Hook Mountain (near Nyack)

Spring Flights: Fair.
Autumn Flights: Good.
Description: An exposed clearing on the summit of a ridge crest.
Access: From the New York Thruway drive north on Route 9W (near Nyack)

for 2 miles. Park in a "dump" on the right side of the road near the bottom of a hill. Walk uphill on Route 9W for about 200 feet to several telephone cable markers and some blue marks painted on the road. Enter the trail to the right and follow the blue trail blazes for a considerable distance to the lookout. The hike requires about 25 minutes and is a very strenuous climb most of the way.

References: California Condor, 1971, 6(3): 13; 1971, 6(4): 12; 1971, 6(5): 10–12.

Jones Beach

Spring Flights: None.
Autumn Flights: Good.
Description: An exposed area near the southwest corner of Zach's Bay between the bay and a fishing station.
Access: From the Long Island Expressway or the Southern State Parkway drive south on the Meadowbrook State Parkway into Jones Beach State Park. Within the park drive east on Ocean Parkway to parking field number four or six (five is closed during autumn) then walk to the

Hook Mountain, N.Y. Photo by D.S. Heintzelman.

7

Zach's Bay area where hawk watching is done.
References: Kingbird, 1958, 8(2): 42–43; 1960, 10(4): 157–59.

Mount Peter (near Greenwood Lake)

Spring Flights: None.
Autumn Flights: Fair.
Description: An exposed rocky outcropping and clearing on a ridge crest.
Access: From Greenwood Lake drive north on Route 17A about 2 miles to the Valley View Restaurant. Park here and walk about 200 feet to the ridge crest behind the restaurant's parking lot.
References: Kingbird, 1967, 17(3): 129–42; 1969, 19(4): 200–203.

New Jersey

Bearfort Mountain (in West Milford Township)

Spring Flights: Fair.
Autumn Flights: Good.
Description: A rocky outcropping near the base of the Bearfort Fire Tower.
Access: From Newfoundland drive north on Route 23 for a mile then turn right onto Union Valley Road. Continue for 5 miles to Stephens Road. Turn left onto Stephens Road and drive for 0.7 mile to a foot path on the left. Park about 150 feet beyond the path then return and follow the path for about 0.5 mile. The lookout rocks are located off the right side of the trail near the fire tower.
References: Urner Field Observer, 1970: 9–21; 1971: 11–17.

Cape May Point

Spring Flights: None.
Autumn Flights: Excellent.
Description: A parking lot beside the lighthouse, exposed areas in front of the lighthouse, or abandoned concrete bunkers along the shoreline. Occasionally other areas are productive and are determined by watching the flight paths of the hawks on any particular day.
Access: Drive south on the Garden State Parkway through Cape May to Cape May Point. Head toward the lighthouse and park in the area beside it. Remain there, walk in front of the lighthouse, or follow the road to the beach where the bunkers are located.
References: Auk, 1936: 393–404; *Bird Studies at Old Cape May* (Dover Publications, 1965).

Cape May Point, N.J. Photo by D.S. Heintzelman.

Catfish Fire Tower (near Blairstown)

Spring Flights: Fair.
Autumn Flights: Fair.
Description: A fire tower placed in a clearing on a forested spur of the Kittatinny Ridge.
Access: From Blairstown drive north for several miles on the Blairstown to Millbrook Road to the point where the Appalachian Trail crosses the highway. This is about 2 miles southwest of Millbrook. Drive southwest along a gravel road (also the trail) as far as possible and park. Continue walking west along the Appalachian Trail about 1.5 miles to the fire tower. Various other trails cross this area but only the Appalachian Trail is marked with white blazes.
Reference: New Jersey Nature News, 1972, 27(1): 19–21.

Montclair Hawk Lookout Sanctuary

Spring Flights: None.
Autumn Flights: Good.
Description: An exposed field overlooking a cliff and quarry.
Access: In Upper Montclair drive west on Bellevue Avenue to Upper Mountain Avenue. Turn right and continue 0.25 mile to Bradford Avenue.

Turn left and drive 0.25 mile to Edgecliff Road (the second street on the right). Continue to the top of the hill and park just before reaching Crestmont Road. Walk east to the lookout on a trail which is entered on the south side of the road.

Reference: Autumn Hawk Flights (Rutgers University Press, 1975).

Raccoon Ridge (near Blairstown)

Spring Flights: Fair.
Autumn Flights: Excellent.
Lookout Description: Two exposed ridge crests on the Kittatinny Ridge.
Access: From Blairstown drive west on Route 94 for several miles to an ice cream stand and a sign pointing to the Yards Creek Pump Storage Station. Drive to the gate of the station, secure permission to enter, and continue to a small picnic area. Park there and walk uphill on a paved road until a spot is reached where powerlines meet the road. Leave the road and walk north along the powerline, cross two small streams, and climb the south slope of the ridge. The last part of this climb is extremely steep and involves vigorous effort. At the top of the ridge walk eastward along the Appalachian Trail for a few hundred feet to an exposed area (the Upper Lookout) identified by several small steel remnants from an old fire tower. Alternatively, after crossing the second stream and beginning to climb the south slope of the ridge, follow an old log road leading to the right of the powerline. Continue on this road generally uphill to the top of the mountain. This brings you to

Montclair Hawk Lookout Sanctuary, N.J. Photo by D.S. Heintzelman.

the Lower Lookout. To visit the Upper Lookout walk west on the Appalachian Trail for about 0.25 mile to the spot described above.
Reference: New Jersey Nature News, 1972, 27(1): 22–28.

North-northeast view from Raccoon Ridge, N.J. Photo by F. Tilly.

Sunrise Mountain

Spring Flights: Fair?
Autumn Flights: Fairly good.
Description: An exposed area on the Appalachian Trail part of which is covered by an open-sided shelter. Unrestricted views are secured toward the south and northwest, but the view northeast is slightly restricted.
Access: From Newton drive north on Route 206 to Stokes State Forest, then follow directional signs to the Sunrise Mountain overlook. Park in the parking lot and walk along a well used trail to the open-sided shelter. The walk requires about five minutes.
Reference: Autumn Hawk Flights (Rutgers University Press, 1975).

Pennsylvania

Bake Oven Knob (near New Tripoli)

Spring Flights: Fair.
Autumn Flights: Excellent.
Description: Two rocky outcroppings on the crest of the Kittatinny Ridge.
The North Lookout (used on westerly and northerly winds) is a small, level
area atop a boulder pile. The South Lookout (used on easterly and southerly
winds) is an exposed rock outcropping terminated by a 1000-foot drop to
the forested slopes below.
Access: At the junction of Routes 309 and 143 at New Tripoli, drive north
on Route 309 for 2 miles. Turn right (east) onto a paved road, continue for
another 2 miles, then turn left onto a paved road running between white
buildings and a house. Continue straight for about 0.25 mile. Do not turn
when the paved road turns sharply right. Instead drive straight ahead on a
gravel road and follow it to the top of the mountain. Park in one of two
parking lots, then walk northeast on the Appalachian Trail for about 0.33
mile to the summit of the Knob. Shortly after crossing a large boulder field
and climbing a steep incline, look for an old cement foundation beside the
trail. The South Lookout is located about 150 feet east of this spot. The North
Lookout is reached by continuing to walk northeastward on the trail for

South Lookout, Bake Oven Knob, Pa. Photo by D.S. Heintzelman.

Bear Rocks, Pa. Photo by D.S. Heintzelman.

about 0.25 mile. After passing a small campsite, walk along the north side of a large boulder pile for about 100 feet, then climb to the top of the boulders to a small, exposed spot at the forward end of the boulder pile. This is the North Lookout.

References: Cassinia, 1969: 11–32; *Autumn Hawk Flights* (Rutgers University Press, 1975).

Bear Rocks (near New Tripoli)

Spring Flights: Fair.
Autumn Flights: Excellent.
Description: A large outcropping of huge boulders on the crest of the Kittatinny Ridge 1.5 miles southwest of Bake Oven Knob.
Access: Drive to the parking lots at Bake Oven Knob. Then walk southwest (in the opposite direction for visiting the Knob) on the Appalachian Trail to a grove of hemlocks and other trees through which the boulder pile can be seen to the right about 200 feet north of the trail. Climb to the top of the boulder pile and select a spot for viewing.
Reference: Autumn Hawk Flights (Rutgers University Press, 1975).

Chickies Rock (near Marietta)

Spring Flights: Fair.
Autumn Flights: Fair.
Description: A 300-foot-high cliff on top of a towering hill overlooking the Susquehanna River. Observers have unrestricted views across the river, upriver, and partly downriver.
Access: From Route 30 at Columbia drive north on Route 441 for 1.1 miles toward Marietta. Park in a large area on the west side of the road just before entering a deep, rocky road cut. Walk west for less than 0.5 mile following a single pole powerline to a split in the trail. Follow the left fork another 300 feet to the lookout.
Reference: None.

Delaware Water Gap

Spring Flights: Fair?
Autumn Flights: Fairly good.
Description: A series of rocky ledges along the Appalachian Trail just before the trail dips into the Gap. One looks across the Gap toward the New Jersey side.
Access: Drive to Tott's Gap from the north side, following directions provided later in this book for that spot, and continue northeastward for several miles on the dirt road which runs along the ridge crest to the Mount Minsi Fire Tower. Park near the tower and walk northeastward on the Appalachian Trail to the rocky ledges overlooking the Gap. The hike from the tower to the ledges requires about five minutes.
References: New Jersey State Museum Science Notes, 1973, 12: 1–3; Autumn Hawk Flights (Rutgers University Press, 1975).

Hawk Mountain Sanctuary (near Kempton)

Spring Flights: Fair.
Autumn Flights: Excellent.
Description: Two rocky outcroppings on the crest of the Kittatinny Ridge. The North Lookout (used on westerly and northerly winds) is atop the main fold of the ridge. The South Lookout (used on easterly and southerly winds)

North Lookout, Hawk Mountain Sanctuary, Pa. Photo by D.S. Heintzelman.

is 500 feet behind the entrance gate on a secondary escarpment.
Access: Drive from Kempton or Drehersville following the directional signs pointing toward the Sanctuary. Park in designated areas and follow the trails to the lookouts. Information can be secured in the headquarters and information center.
References: Hawks Aloft: The Story of Hawk Mountain (Dodd, Mead, 1949); *Feathers in the Wind* (Hawk Mountain Sanctuary, 1973).

Tott's Gap (near Delaware Water Gap)

Spring Flights: Poor?
Autumn Flights: Fair.
Description: A pipeline right-of-way crossing the Kittatinny Ridge and providing a clear view north and south from the ridge crest.
Access: In Delaware Water Gap, Pennsylvania, follow the Cherry Valley Road to the edge of a golf course, then turn left (west) onto the Poplar Valley Road and continue for several miles to the Tott's Gap Road. Turn left and follow the Tott's Gap Road to the top of the mountain. At the top turn left (northeast) and follow the dirt road for about 0.25 mile, past a communications facility, to a radio tower and the pipeline right-of-way. The pipeline is marked by a white steel post beside the road. When westerly and northerly winds occur remain near the radio tower and look north over the pipeline cut. On easterly and southerly winds walk south along the pipeline for a few

hundred feet to an exposed area and observe from there over the valley south of the ridge.

References: New Jersey State Museum Science Notes, 1973, 12: 1–3; *Autumn Hawk Flights* (Rutgers University Press, 1975).

Tuscarora Mountain (near Chambersburg)

Spring Flights: None.

Autumn Flights: Fair.

Description: A flat, exposed area on top of a large pile of rocks named The Pulpit.

Access: From Chambersburg drive west on Route 30 toward McConnellsburg. Park at an inn at the top of Tuscarora Mountain and follow the sign marked for The Pulpit.

Reference: Autumn Hawk Flights (Rutgers University Press, 1975).

Waggoner's Gap (near Carlisle)

Spring Flights: None.

Autumn Flights: Good.

Description: A partly exposed boulder pile (used on westerly and northerly winds) on the crest of the Kittatinny Ridge. Alternatively (on easterly and southerly winds) the shoulder of a mountain road.

Access: Drive north on Route 74 from Carlisle to the top of the Kittatinny Ridge. Park near a communications tower. Either remain along the roadside near the tower or cross the highway and walk across a parking lot and follow a path for about 150 feet to the lookout on the boulder pile.

References: Atlantic Naturalist, 1966, 21: 161–68; *Autumn Hawk Flights* (Rutgers University Press, 1975).

Waggoner's Gap, Pa. Photo by D.S. Heintzelman.

8

Maryland

Assateague Island National Seashore

Spring Flights: None?
Autumn Flights: Good.
Description: The dunes and outer beach areas along the length of the island are famous as a Peregrine Falcon flyway.
Access: There are two entrances to Assateague Island National Seashore. To reach the northern entrance drive west on Route 50 from Ocean City to the junction of Route 611. Turn onto Route 611 and continue south for a few miles until park signs and an unnumbered road leading east into the park are encountered. The southern entrance (located in Virginia) is reached from Pocomoke City, Maryland, by driving south on Route 13 to Route 175, then turning east onto Route 175 and following it into the park.
References: Raptor Research News, 1971, 5: 31–43; *Journal Wildlife Management,* 1972, 36: 484–92.

Monument Knob State Park (near Boonsboro)

Spring Flights: None.
Autumn Flights: Good.
Description: The roof of a stone tower in the park.
Access: From Boonsboro follow alternate (old) Route 40 to the top of South Mountain then turn north onto a road opposite an inn and continue for a mile to Washington Monument State Park. Enter the park and drive to a parking lot near the stone tower. Walk to the tower via a trail and climb to the top. Observe from there.
References: Atlantic Naturalist, 1951, 6: 166–68; 1966, 21: 161–68.

Delaware

Brandywine Creek State Park (near Wilmington)

Spring Flights: None?
Autumn Flights: Fair.
Description: A stone wall overlooking the Brandywine Creek and adjacent to the main parking lot in the park.
Access: From Wilmington, 3 miles to the south, drive north on Route 100 to the junction with Route 92. Enter the park then continue to the main parking lot and to the stone wall adjacent to it. Observe from here.
Reference: Delaware Conservationist, 1969, 13(4): 3–13.

Observation tower, Monument Knob State Park, Md. Photo by D.S. Heintzelman.

Virginia

Kiptopeke

Spring Flights: None.
Autumn Flights: Good.
Description: The tip of the Delmarva peninsula about a mile south of the town of Kiptopeke.
Access: From Norfolk to the south, or more northern points on the Delmarva peninsula, follow Route 13 to the southern end of the peninsula and look for local directional signs pointing to Kiptopeke.
Reference: Autumn Hawk Flights (Rutgers University Press, 1975).

Mendota Fire Tower (near Hansonville)

Spring Flights: None.
Autumn Flights: Good.
Description: A fire tower providing exposed views from the summit of Clinch Mountain.
Access: From Abingdon drive north on Route 19 (Alt. 58) to Hansonville, then follow Route 802 to Route 614 and continue to the top of the mountain. Park in the saddle at the top and hike on the trail on the right for about 15 minutes until the fire tower is reached.
Reference: Autumn Hawk Flights (Rutgers University Press, 1975).

West Virginia

Bear Rocks (adjacent to Monongahela National Forest)

Spring Flights: None.
Autumn Flights: Good.
Description: A rocky outcropping on the Allegheny Front overlooking the Dolly Sods Scenic Area.

Mendota Fire Tower, Va. Photo by T. Swindell.

Access: From the Dolly Sods Scenic Area in Monongahela National Forest drive north on Forest Service Road 75 past the Red Creek Camp Ground to Bear Rocks. This is located just outside of the national forest boundary. Park and walk to the rocky outcropping used as a lookout.
Reference: Autumn Hawk Flights (Rutgers University Press, 1975).

Hanging Rocks Fire Tower (near Waiteville)

Spring Flights: None.
Autumn Flights: Good.
Description: A fire tower built on a rocky outcropping on the crest of Peters Mountain.
Access: By road about 3 miles northwest of Waiteville. From Route 311 in Paint Bush, Virginia, drive west on county route 600 for 11 miles to Waiteville, West Virginia, then turn right onto a dirt road and continue 3.6 miles up Peters Mountain to a dirt road on the left. Turn onto the road and park in a suitable spot. Then hike *uphill* along a trail leading toward the top of the mountain. Turn left at a "tee" in the trail near some buildings and shortly thereafter climb a steep bank to a field. Follow the trail over the left side of the field and enter the forest on the left side via a narrow trail (sometimes somewhat overgrown at the entrance for the first few hundred feet). Follow this trail for about 0.5 mile until the fire tower is reached.
Reference: Redstart, 1970, 37(3): 82–86.

Bear Rocks, W. Va. Photo by D.S. Heintzelman.

Southern Appalachian States

Although some hawk watching has been done in the southern Appalachian states, particularly in Tennessee, sufficient details are unavailable on most sites suitable as lookouts in this region to allow a full discussion here. Hence information in this section is of a preliminary and incomplete nature. Observers in this region can make valuable contributions to ornithological knowledge by conducting sufficiently adequate field studies of hawk flights from individual sites (usually for the duration of a season) to evaluate the importance of a site as a concentration point and migration flight line. Detailed access directions permitting readers to visit the site should be included in the published reports which should follow such field studies.

Tennessee

Dunlap Fire Tower (near Chattanooga)

Spring Flights: None.
Autumn Flights: Fair.
Description: A fire tower on Walden Ridge where Route 127 crosses the time-zone boundary.
Access: From Chattanooga drive north on Route 127 to Walden Ridge. The tower is located beside the highway and is readily accessible.
Reference: Autumn Hawk Flights (Rutgers University Press, 1975).

Fall Creek Falls State Park (near Spencer)

Spring Flights: None.
Autumn Flights: Fair.
Description: A fire tower in the state park, on the Cumberland Plateau.
Access: From Pikeville drive northwest on Route 30 for several miles to Fall Creek Falls State Park. Enter the park and continue to the fire tower from which hawk watching is done.
Reference: Migrant, 1949, 20(1): 16.

Rogersville-Kyles Ford Fire Tower (near Edison)

Spring Flights: None.
Autumn Flights: Good.
Description: A fire tower on the crest of Clinch Mountain.
Access: From Rogersville drive north on Route 70 to the summit of Clinch Mountain. The fire tower, which can be seen from the road, is located on the ridge east of the highway. Park along the east side of the highway, then hike for about ten minutes until the tower is reached.
Reference: Autumn Hawk Flights (Rutgers University Press, 1975).

Kentucky

Although hawks migrate across Kentucky, only very limited information is available regarding consistently used concentration points and flight lines. In *The Birds of Kentucky* (American Ornithologists' Union, 1965), however, Robert M. Mengel mentions that Red-tailed Hawks migrate down the Mississippi Valley in early November.

North Carolina

Information on hawk flights in North Carolina is too limited to provide full details on suitable hawk lookouts, but some cursory comments are possible. Along the state's inland mountains various spots along the Blue Ridge Parkway — the area between Little Switzerland, Mount Mitchell, and Thunder Hill — have produced hawk flights in the past. Other Blue Ridge Parkway sites from which hawk flights have been reported include Blowing Rock, Doughton Park, and Roaring Gap. Table Rock, on the eastern edge of the Blue Ridge, also is used as a hawk lookout occasionally.

Coastal North Carolina also is used as an autumn hawk flyway. Sharp-shinned and Cooper's Hawks pass the vicinity of Nags Head, and Peregrine Falcons migrate along the Outer Banks. Migrating Ospreys also have been reported in early October over Topsail Island near New River inlet.

Florida

From time to time, particularly during autumn, migrating hawks have been observed crossing portions of Florida. Some notable flights of Broad-winged Hawks have been reported in the Key West area, and some migrating hawks also have been observed over the Dry Tortugas. More consistent flights seem to occur, however, on Upper Plantation Key outside the offices of the National Audubon Society Research Department, 115 Indian Mound Trail, Travernier, and at Gulf Breeze in the northwestern section of the state.

Gulf Breeze

Spring Flights: None.
Autumn Flights: Fair.
Description: The side of a road at a sharp curve.
Access: From Pensacola drive south on Route 98 into Gulf Breeze. Continue to the traffic light (the only one in town), turn west at the light onto Fairpoint Drive, and continue for 1.7 miles until the road curves sharply toward the southeast. Observe from the roadside in the vicinity of the curve. Hawks approach from the east.
Reference: J. Hawk Migration Assn. North America, 1975, 1(1): 30, 32.

Appendix 1
Raptor Conservation Organizations

In addition to the well-known national conservation organizations, all of
which support preservation of birds of prey, the following organizations
are especially concerned with raptor conservation.

Hawk Migration Association of North America
c/o Hawk Mountain Sanctuary
R.D. 2
Kempton, Pa. 19529

Hawk Mountain Sanctuary Association
R.D. 2
Kempton, Pa. 19529

Raptor Research Foundation, Inc.
c/o Biology Department
University of South Dakota
Vermillion, S.D. 57069

Society for the Preservation of Birds of Prey
Pacific Palisades, Calif. 90272

Appendix 2

HAWK MIGRATION DATA SHEET

Date: _____ Observers: _____

Location: _____

Time (E.S.T.)	7-8	8-9	9-10	10-11	11-12	12-1	1-2	2-3	3-4	4-5	5-6	6-7	Totals
Max. Vis. (Miles)													
Air Temp.													
Wind Speed (MPH)													
Wind Direction													
% Cloud Cover													
Turkey Vulture													
Goshawk													
Sharp-shinned Hawk													
Cooper's Hawk													
Red-tailed Hawk													
Red-shouldered Hawk													
Broad-winged Hawk													
Rough-legged Hawk													
Golden Eagle													
Bald Eagle													
Marsh Hawk													
Osprey													
Peregrine Falcon													
Pigeon Hawk													
Sparrow Hawk													
Unidentified Hawk													
Totals													

NOTES:

Date_____ Area_____ Observers_____

Time (E.S.T.)	7-8			8-9			9-10			10-11			11-12			12-1			Totals		
Visibility																					
Air Temp.																					
Bar. Pressure																					
Cloud Cover (%)																					
Wind Direction																					
Wind Velocity																					
	A	I	U	A	I	U	A	I	U	A	I	U	A	I	U	A	I	U	A	I	U
Red-tailed																					
Red-shouldered																					
Broad-winged																					
	D	L	U	D	L	U	D	L	U	D	L	U	D	L	U	D	L	U	D	L	U
Rough-legged																					
Goshawk																					
Cooper's																					
Sharp-shinned																					
Peregrine																					
Pigeon Hawk																					
	M	F	U	M	F	U	M	F	U	M	F	U	M	F	U	M	F	U	M	F	U
Sparrow Hawk																					
Golden Eagle																					
Bald Eagle																					
Osprey																					
Marsh Hawk																					
Unidentified																					
Totals																					
Visitors																					

Notes: (PLEASE KEEP RECORDS OF ALL SMALL BIRDS)

AFTERNOON

Date _____ Area _____ Observers _____

	1-2			2-3			3-4			4-5			5-6			6-7			Totals		
Time (E.S.T.)	A	I	U	A	I	U	A	I	U	A	I	U	A	I	U	A	I	U	A	I	U
Visibility																					
Air Temp.																					
Bar. Pressure																					
Cloud Cover (%)																					
Wind Direction																					
Wind Velocity																					
	A	I	U	A	I	U	A	I	U	A	I	U	A	I	U	A	I	U	A	I	U
Red-tailed																					
Red-shouldered																					
Broad-winged																					
	D	L	U	D	L	U	D	L	U	D	L	U	D	L	U	D	L	U	D	L	U
Rough-legged																					
Goshawk																					
Cooper's																					
Sharp-shinned																					
	M	F	U	M	F	U	M	F	U	M	F	U	M	F	U	M	F	U	M	F	U
Peregrine																					
Pigeon Hawk																					
Sparrow Hawk																					T
Golden Eagle																					
Bald Eagle																					
Osprey																					
Marsh Hawk																					
Unidentified																					
Totals																					
Visitors																					

Notes: (PLEASE KEEP RECORDS OF ALL SMALL BIRDS)

Report by: _____ {(a.m.) (p.m.)}　　　MONTCLAIR BIRD CLUB - DAILY HAWK COUNT　　　Date: _____

Time	Buteos			Accipiters		Falcons			Other			Un	Total
	BW	RT	RS	SS	CH	Sp H	DH	PH	OS	MH	BE		
-9													
9-10													
10-11													
11-12													
12-1													
1-2													
2-3													
3-4													
4-5													
5+													
Total													

Selected Reading

Bent, Arthur Cleveland. 1937. *Life Histories of North American Birds of Prey*. Part 1. United States National Museum Bulletin 167. Reprint. New York: Dover Publications
———— 1938. *Life Histories of North American Birds of Prey*. Part 2. United States National Museum Bulletin 170. Reprint. New York: Dover Publications
Brett, James J. and Alexander C. Nagy. 1973. *Feathers in the Wind*. Kempton, Pa.: Hawk Mountain Sanctuary Association
Broun, Maurice. 1949. *Hawks Aloft: The Story of Hawk Mountain*. New York: Dodd, Mead (out of print)
Brown, Leslie and Dean Amadon. 1968. *Eagles, Hawks and Falcons of the World*. 2 vols. New York: McGraw-Hill
Harwood, Michael. 1973. *The View from Hawk Mountain*. New York: Scribner's
Hawk Migration Association of North America. 1975. *Proceedings of the North American Hawk Migration Conference 1974*. Washington Depot, Conn.: Shiver Mountain Press (obtain from the association)
Heintzelman, Donald S. 1970. *The Hawks of New Jersey*. New Jersey State Museum Bulletin 13
————. 1972. *A Guide to Northeastern Hawk Watching*. Lambertville, N.J.: Published Privately (out of print)
————.1975. *Autumn Hawk Flights: The Migrations in Eastern North America*. New Brunswick, N.J.: Rutgers University Press
May, John Bichard. 1935. *The Hawks of North America*. New York: National Association of Audubon Societies (out of print)
Peterson, Roger Tory, 1947. *A Field Guide to the Birds*. 2d rev. ed. Boston: Houghton Mifflin
Porter, R. F., Ian Willis, Steen Christensen, and Bent Pors Nielsen. 1974. *Flight Identification of European Raptors*. Berkhamsted, England: Poyser
Pough, Richard H. 1951. *Audubon Water Bird Guide: Water, Game and Large Land Birds*. New York: Doubleday
Robbins, Chandler S. et al. 1966. *A Guide to Field Identification/Birds of North America*. New York: Golden Press
Stone, Witmer. 1937. *Bird Studies at Old Cape May*. 2 vols. Delaware Valley Ornithological Club, Philadelphia, Pa. Reprint. New York: Dover Publications

Index

Page numbers in bold-faced type refer to the illustrations.

Acadia National Park (Me.), 70
Accipiter cooperii, 11, **25**
   gentilis, 11, **23-24**
   striatus, 11, **26-28**
American Kestrel, 16, **50-52**
Aquila chrysaetos, 14, **41**
Assateague Island National Seashore
   (Md.), 86
Autumn hawk migrations, 55

Bake Oven Knob (Pa.), 80-81
Bald Peak (Conn.), 73
Bearfort Mountain (N.J.), 76
Bear Rocks (Pa.), 82
Bear Rocks (W.Va.), 88-89
Binoculars, 53
Blue Ridge Parkway (N.C.), 91
Braddock Bay State Park (N.Y.), 67
Brandywine Creek State Park (Del.), 86
Brier Island (N.S.), 69
Buteo brachyurus, 13, **36**
   jamaicensis, 12, **29-31**
   lagopus, 13, **37-38**
   lineatus, 12, **32**
   platypterus, 12, **33-35**
   swainsoni, 13, **36**

Cape May Point (N.J.), 76
Caracara, 15, **47**
Caracara cheriway, 15, **47**
Casco Bay Area (Me.), 70
Catfish Fire Tower (N.J.), 77
Cathartes aura, 9, **18-19**
Cedar Grove Ornithological Station
   (Wisc.), 63
Chickies Rock (Pa.), 82
Circus cyaneus, 14, **42-44**
Conneaut (Ohio), 64
Coragyps atratus, 9, **20**

Delaware Water Gap (Pa.), 82
Derby Hill (N.Y.), 67
Diversion-lines, 60-61
Dry Tortugas (Fla.), 91
Dunlap Fire Tower (Tenn.), 90

Eagles
   Bald, 14, **39-40**
   Golden, 14, **41**
Elanoides forficatus, 10, **21**
Elanus leucurus, 10, **21**
Equipment, 53-54

Falco columbarius, 16, **50**
   peregrinus, 16, **49**
   rusticolus, 15-16, **48**
   sparverius, 16, **50-52**

Falcons
   American Kestrel, 16, **50-52**
   Gyrfalcon, 15-16, **48**
   Merlin, 16
   Peregrine, 16, **49**
Fall Creek Falls State Park (Tenn.), 90
Field clothing, 53-54
Field equipment, 53-54
Fire Island (N.Y.), 74
· Fishers Island (N.Y.), 74

Gulf Breeze (Fla.), 91

Haliaeetus leucocephalus, 14, **39-40**
Hanging Rocks Fire Tower (W.Va.), 89
Hawk Cliff (Ont.), 67
Hawk Mountain Sanctuary (Pa.), 82-83
Hawk Ridge Nature Reserve (Minn.), 62
Hawks
   Broad-winged, 12, **33-35**
   Cooper's, 11, **25**
   Goshawk, 11, **23-24**
   Marsh, 14, **42-44**
   Red-shouldered, 12, **32**
   Red-tailed, 12, **29-31**
   Rough-legged, 13, **37-38**
   Sharp-shinned, 11, **26-28**
   Short-tailed, 13, **36**
   Swainson's, 13, **36**
Hogback Mountain (Vt.), 71
Holiday Beach, Provincial Park (Ont.),
   68
Hook Mountain (N.Y.), 74-75

Ictinia misisippiensis, 10, **22**

Jones Beach (N.Y.), 75-76

Key West (Fla.), 91
Kiptopeke (Va.), 87
Kites
   Everglade, 11, **22**
   Mississippi, 10, **22**
   Swallow-tailed, 10, **21**
   White-tailed, 10, **21**

Lakewood Park (Ohio), 64
Lighthouse Point (Conn.), 73
Little Round Top (N.H.), 70-71

Martha's Vineyard (Mass.), 72
Mechanics of hawk flights, 58-61
Mendota Fire Tower (Va.), 88
Merlin, 16, **50**
Migration seasons, 55-56
Montclair Hawk Lookout Sanctuary
   (N.J.), 77-78

Monument Knob State Park (Md.), 86
Mount Peter (N.Y.), 76
Mount Tom State Reservation (Mass.), 72

Nags Head (N.C.), 91

Osprey, 15, **45-47**
Outer Banks (N.C.), 91

Pandion haliaetus, 15, **45-47**
Peaked Hill (N.H.), 71
Perkins Beach (Ohio), 64
Point Pelee National Park (Ont.), 69
Port Credit (Ont.), 68-69
Presque Isle State Park (Pa.), 66

Raccoon Ridge (N.J.), 70
Rogersville-Kyles Ford Fire Tower
   (Tenn.), 90
Rostrhamus sociabilis, 11, **22**

Spring hawk migrations, 55
Straits of Mackinac (Mich.), 63
Sunrise Mountain (N.J.), 79

Table Rock (N.C.), 91
Telescopes, 53
Thermals, 59-60
Topsail Island (N.C.), 91
Tott's Gap (Pa.), 83-84
Tuscarora Mountain (Pa.), 84

Uncanoonuc Mountain (N.H.), 71
Updrafts, 59

Vultures
   Black, 9, **20**
   Turkey, 9, **18-19**

Waggoner's Gap (Pa.), 84
Weather conditions, 58
West Lake Junior High School (Pa.), 66
Whitefish Point (Mich.), 63